Couponing Guide

340 Great Tips to Get Free or Cheap Groceries Using Coupons

By Adam Gold

Published by Liraz Publishing

www.BizMove.com

340 Great Tips to Get Free or Cheap Groceries Using Coupons

A decade ago, most shoppers clipped the occasional coupon that afforded them a whopping 15-cent discount on creamed corn or toilet tissue. These days, however, couponing has become a way of life for many. If you want to get the most from your couponing adventures, read on, and learn the ins and outs of successful couponing.

Please note that a few of the tips in this book repeat themselves. It is done intentionally as research shows that this may help you better remember the advice provided in this book.

Tips start here:

Only use coupons for products that you will actually use. You won't save any money by purchasing items that your family does not need or brands that you don't like just because you have a coupon. Cutting out coupons for items you don't use also costs you time, which could be better spent.

Make sure you understand and print off coupon policies for your local stores. Walmart, for example, has a printable coupon policy. Keep them in your coupon organizer for handy usage. On occasion, a cashier may not know the corporate policies for their stores, and having the policy may help you get the leg up in a disagreement.

Check coupons online to see if there are any coupons available for items you need. If you find a coupon for an item, you need, look at the store's flyer and see if there are any sales on the item. If there aren't, check the price when you go to the store.

To get extra circulars from the Sunday papers, make inquiries with the publisher about couponer's price breaks. They may have a deal if you subscribe and order a certain number of Sunday papers each week.

Don't forget about online coupons. Traditional paper coupons are great, but there are tons of great coupons online. There are various coupon sites that you can join too. Receiving instant notifications to your inbox can help you get access to many deals before other people. Some sites also have promo codes that can help you boost your savings.

Do not buy something just because you have a coupon for it. Many extreme couponers will only buy an item because they have a coupon for it; this can make you waste tons of money. Instead, hold onto the coupon and when the item is on sale, use it then.

Read the small print of a coupon. For instance, you may get a coupon for a dollar off your favorite food. But when you see the fine print, you may realize you have to buy two to save the dollar. It can be hassle to get to the checkout only to figure out it is not such a good deal after all.

If you carry a loyalty card for a particular store, check the store's website for coupons. Many retailers offer manufacturer's coupons on their website and allow you to download them to your card. Your stored coupons are automatically deducted when the cashier swipes your card at the cash register.

Don't only look to print papers, look to the Internet as well. Many websites contain coupons that you can print and bring with you. Some even have digital coupons that you can scan from your smart phone while in the store. Or if you are online shopping, they may provide a coupon code for your use.

Use every medium available to collect your coupons. You can find them locally in newspapers, mailers and on receipts. They are also available online on store websites, manufacturers' websites, Facebook, Twitter and on a specific coupon-collecting sites. Always keep your eyes open for coupons to save the most money.

Shop at the store with the most sales. Go where your coupons take you. Don't just stick to one store. By doing most of your shopping in one place, you are likely to be missing out on some great deals. To save the most money, get out of your comfort zone and shop around.

Find a website that will consolidate coupon offers from a variety of sites to get the most coupons. This saves you a lot of time in your efforts to save lots of money.

Purge old or unwanted coupons from your collection routinely. Keeping your coupon stash filled with expired coupons is a waste of time and money since the clutter keeps you from finding the coupons that are most useful to you. Make it a point to clean out expired coupons every week or so.

Start your coupon collecting with only one store. Coupons may seem like an easy thing to collect and utilize, but there are many complexities. Some coupons have multiple policies. Some stores allow coupons from competitors. Some stores will even accept coupons that have expired - even months after the expiration date.

Keep in mind that you might end up with 40 sticks of free deodorant or 100 bottles of shampoo on your shelf. If you want to stock up, this is great but if you do not have the space, you will always want to keep this in mind and steer clear of these traps.

Where do you find coupons that will save you some serious money? First, look in your local newspaper, and next print them from home by searching online according to your shopping list. It's amazing what you can find when you search for coupons online. You will find yourself saving money on just about everything.

If you can, shop at places that offer the doubling of coupons. The potential for increased savings is significant, and there are a surprising number of stores that offer this. In the right circumstances, coupon doubling can even make products totally free of charge. Things that are free are the best! You may want to also think about getting new products that you haven't tried yet.

A good coupon tip you can use is to sort you coupons by their expiration date. Organizing your coupons this way will make it so that you get the most out of your coupons and you won't waste any of them. It will make your shopping get done much smoother.

To find some of the best deals, join couponing blogs. These blogs offer not only methods to find the best coupons, but many will also tell you what stores have the lowest prices to begin with. These match-ups will help you figure out where the cheapest place is to shop.

One method of securing coupons easily is taking advantage of the Sunday newspaper. Sunday papers almost always have coupons, unless it is a Sunday before a major holiday. Different newspapers have different coupons, so get a local one as well as the newspaper for the closest metropolitan city to ensure you have a range of coupons.

Take advantage of the grocery store competition

and use the coupon strategies to your advantage. Many stores may be willing to accept competitor coupons. When you take advantage of these deals, it helps you to save time and money from having to travel around to many different stores. You can unknowingly cancel out your cost savings in fuel costs by driving around too much.

Think before you click the submit button! Always do an online search for coupon codes before making an online purchase. There are even whole websites dedicated to keeping databases of coupon codes. Visit retailmenot.com or couponcabin.com before making a purchase. It only takes a second and could save you a lot of money.

Keep all your coupons in one place. Some coupons are really small, and you don't want to lose them. You also don't want to have coupons all over the house. When you keep them all in one place, you can locate them when you need them without too much trouble.

Use store coupons along with manufacturer coupons. Most stores will allow you to use one of their coupons along with a manufacturer coupon; utilize this technique for extreme savings. Many stores will honor both coupons; however, when utilizing this savings strategy have a printed copy of the store's coupon policy.

A good tip if you like to use coupons is not to get carried away with simply clipping out coupons. Only keep coupons that you intend to use. If something is on sale that you're unlikely to buy, then you should just leave it. Time is also money so you don't want to waste more than you have to.

Coupon clipping services are a great way to save more. These services allow you to access coupons throughout the country, and may have a higher value than those offered in your area for the same products. Research services that are consumer friendly and offer a quick turn around on your coupons.

Make friends with the cashiers. Particularly if you are in the same stores fairly often, it is important to be polite and thank them whenever possible. They can really help the process go much smoother if they aren't annoyed at having to scan all your coupons. A little personality can go a long way.

When you enter any store check the front to see if you can find their weekly paper. In their weekly paper, a lot of shops will offer you coupons inside of them to help entice you to purchase more things at their store. This can work in your favor, and you can find a lot of items for cheap through their coupons.

Familiarize yourself with common coupon acronyms. "BOGO" is an acronym used to indicate that if you buy one, you will get one free. If a coupon says 'MIR,' that is the same as saying that you can mail in a form to get a rebate. So be on the look for more acronyms so that you have a good amount of knowledge about them. When you are unaware of these acronyms, you might just miss out on great deals, and even greater deals via your coupons.

The key to couponing is having all of your coupons organized and easy to retrieve. Coupons can be organized by category. There are many other ways to organize your coupons including by expiration date or by your store's layout. You will enjoy couponing the most when things are organized and easy to manage.

Many stores have an online store, and you can sign up for notifications when they have a sale. You can also check the site for current coupon offers periodically. You can print the coupon from their website, or use the code they provide if you want to order an item online.

When using coupons, it is important to recognize that small amounts of money add up over time into large amounts. Coupon savings of only 10 or 25 cents may not seem like very much, but you would be surprised at just how much money these small value coupons will end up saving you over your life time. Save little to save big.

Talk to your friends or neighbors to see if you can trade coupons with them. Go over all of the coupons that you have found and ask someone else if they can trade with you. By doing this you can help each other out and save a bunch of money as well.

Make sure you use the coupons you have in conjunction with a store that has good sales. Check the store's weekly flyer before going there. No matter what coupons you use, if the store does not have good sales, you are not getting the best deal possible. If one store does not have good sales, check another store.

If you do your online research, there are several couponing websites you can go to find the best deals on coupons on all of your favorite items. You may even be able to clip that coupon that will get you some free items to have you saving a whole lot at the checkout.

Just because you have a coupon does not mean that it will give you the best price for a product. Many times, the generic or store brand equivalent will still be a better buy than the product on the face of the coupon. Don't always believe that a coupon will have you saving the most amount of money.

Go to the website of your favorite grocery store to find out what kind of weekly specials they may have and then go through your coupon book to see if you can get any extra deals. The coupon websites do not always have everything listed. You might find a great deal on your own.

When you have a manufacturer's coupon, you can stack that coupon with store coupons. This is a great way to get items for next to free or almost free. Use the store's coupons from their weekly circular and match them up with coupons from the manufacturer off the Internet or from the newspaper.

Try to clip coupons for every item you find, even if you do not use that product. Sometimes you may have a neighbor who needs coupons for diapers, and you could trade them the diaper coupons for ones that you can use. This helps you and your neighbor as well.

Get organized with your coupons. Use a three ring binder with baseball card holders to sort them. Separate the coupons into different sections, such as dairy, baking products, frozen, and others. Keep a section open for coupons you plan to use immediately. That way, when you get to the store, you are ready to go.

The best way to keep all of your coupons in order is to buy some plastic inserts and keep them in a binder. You can buy different sizes of plastic pouches and perhaps keep them in categories this way. You can organize it. However, will be easiest for you to get through.

Take advantage of any reward's cards programs that your local grocery store provides. Often times the store will allow you to load certain coupons right onto your card. This is so nice because you do not have to clip them out, but you also have to remember to note what you put on the card so that you are sure what you need to buy. Furthermore, you cannot use more than one coupon at a time, and they often limit doubling.

A great tip you can try if you like to use coupons is to do some comparing from coupons of different stores. This is a good way to find the very best deal. Some stores will even match a competitor's price, which means you won't have to travel all over to different stores.

Buy more than one Sunday newspaper. Generally, it is recommended that a family should buy the same number of newspapers as they have family members. You can use these coupons to buy the many different items your family uses on a regular basis. If you don't use all the coupons, share them.

Use every medium available to collect your coupons. You can find them locally in newspapers, mailers and on receipts. They are also available online on store websites, manufacturers' websites, Facebook, Twitter and on a specific coupon-collecting sites. Always keep your eyes open for coupons to save the most money.

If you really want to succeeding at couponing, install a toolbar for search engines on your browser. Before making any online purchase, look for promo codes and coupons. There are deals waiting for you that cover a broad range of categories.

When you are trying to acquire the best coupons, one of the things that you will need to do is make sure that they are not expired. The worst thing that you can do is spend unnecessary time cutting out coupons that are no longer valid to use on your purchase.

Hold on to your coupons. Many times coupons will run in conjunction with a "sale" at a local store to entice you to use the coupon immediately. It may seem like a good deal, but if you hold on to the coupon, more often than not, the product price will drop even lower before the coupon expires. A little bit of extra patience will score you a bigger deal!

It is important to have your coupons organized, to avoid expiration dates passing without your knowledge. In addition to sorting by type, put the ones with the soonest expiration dates first. When you see that the time is approaching, add the item to your shopping list. Knowing what you have in advance will also help you to work with the in-store sales.

Use a system for keeping your coupons tidy and organized. Envelopes, binders or expandable files are all great tools. Not only, being organized keep you from forgetting to use your coupons, but it saves time at the register. Preparing ahead of time keeps you from having to dig for and sort coupons while checking out, leading to quick grocery trips.

To get coupons for brands you particularly enjoy, all you have to do is ask. Many companies are willing to send out coupons to people who email or write to them. Simply send a letter noting how much you enjoy a product and ask if they would provide you with coupons. You will be surprised at how often they oblige!

When you have a manufacturer's coupon, you can stack that coupon with store coupons. This is a great way to get items for next to free or almost free. Use the store's coupons from their weekly circular and match them up with coupons from the manufacturer off the Internet or from the newspaper.

To maximize your savings when using coupons, use

them to purchase items that are on sale and at supermarkets that offer double or triple coupon savings. When you buy an item that is on sale and use a coupon that is doubled or tripled, you may find that you pay pennies for the item or even get it for free!

Think before you click the submit button! Always do an online search for coupon codes before making an online purchase. There are even whole websites dedicated to keeping databases of coupon codes. Visit retailmenot.com or couponcabin.com before making a purchase. It only takes a second and could save you a lot of money.

Internet forums are a great source for discovering great offers. There are many sites where people share information about money saving coupons. Printing coupons is not the only perk, as these sites will often also tell you how well the codes and coupons have worked for others.

Check coupons online to see if there are any coupons available for items you need. If you find a coupon for an item, you need, look at the store's flyer and see if there are any sales on the item. If there aren't, check the price when you go to the store.

Don't forget about online coupons. Traditional paper coupons are great, but there are tons of great coupons online. There are various coupon sites that you can join too. Receiving instant notifications to your inbox can help you get access to many deals before other people. Some sites also have promo codes that can help you boost your savings.

Request all the free sample offers you can find. Not only will you get the free sample in the mail, but often times you'll receive a coupon for the item as well. Coupons that come with free samples tend to be higher value than others, so you'll get a great sample and a great deal!

Organize your coupons so that you can find them faster when you need them. Special coupon organizers are available for purchase that allows you to organize your coupons in various categories. This makes it easier to locate just the coupon you need without searching through your entire trove of coupons.

When you are cutting coupons you should make sure you have a filing system that is labeled for each different grocery department. This will make it easier to find your coupons when you are planning a big shopping trip once per week. You will save a lot of time by doing this.

If you are clipping coupons, add a binder to your list of supplies. A binder is a great way to store and organize your coupons, and you can carry it with you every time you shop. Having it on hand will help to ensure that you use the coupons you clip and save money.

Shop at stores that multiply coupons. Some stores double or triple coupons everyday. Other stores have certain days on which they will multiply manufacturer coupons. Be sure to read the fine print, because some stores just allow a limited number to be multiplied, require a minimum purchase, or only multiply coupons with lower values.

Before getting your car serviced anywhere, check their website first. Many mechanics and service centers have a page for current deals and coupons that you can print out and use. These might be national deals, or just ones running at that particular location. It only takes a minute to check and can save you a few bucks.

A good coupon tip you should use is to do all of your shopping at the end of the month. Most stores have it so that their coupons expire at the end of the month. Shopping during this time will make it more convenient for you to get the best deals.

Shop at the store with the most sales. Go where your coupons take you. Don't just stick to one store. By doing most of your shopping in one place, you are likely to be missing out on some great deals. To save the most money, get out of your comfort zone and shop around.

You may know to subscribe to the Sunday paper; however, you should also subscribe to magazines that offer coupons. Check online for circulars that are popular within the couponing community. Often, these magazines will have garnered great coupons that are hard to find, if not impossible to find, anywhere else.

Check the packaging and contents thoroughly of everything you buy and use before you throw it away or recycle it. You never know where you might find a coupon. Sometimes they are hiding on the bottom of a box, or have slipped down to the bottom of the inside of one.

Clip coupons and then shop online. Many online retailers will accept manufacturer coupons, which means big savings for you. Because of the low overhead with an online store, costs can be reduced, thus saving you more. Many times this can be like doubling your coupon savings, which is always a treat.

Figure out what the policy is on using coupons at stores you're going to. You want to know if you can double or triple your coupons or how strict their expiration policy is. Gather as much information as possible to garner the highest possible savings.

Go to the website of your favorite grocery store to find out what kind of weekly specials they may have and then go through your coupon book to see if you can get any extra deals. The coupon websites do not always have everything listed. You might find a great deal on your own.

Look for ways to double up sales with coupons. Sometimes, this means that you will have to hang onto a coupon for a couple of weeks instead of using it on your next shopping trip. This may also mean that you will need to make more shopping trips, but the money you save will be worth the trouble.

Use the Internet to your advantage. As couponing has become more popular, more and more websites are offering coupons that you can just print out at home. Frequent these sites, and check them often. These coupons are free and snagging them often does not require a large time investment either.

Try to clip coupons for every item you find, even if you do not use that product. Sometimes you may have a neighbor who needs coupons for diapers, and you could trade them the diaper coupons for ones that you can use. This helps you and your neighbor as well.

Don't rely on just one paper or website to get coupons from. Try subscribing to several sources if you can. You can even ask friends and family for their unused papers. The more sources you have in your arsenal, the more deals you have access to so that you can save money.

Organize your coupons so that you can find them faster when you need them. Special coupon organizers are available for purchase that allows you to organize your coupons in various categories. This makes it easier to locate just the coupon you need without searching through your entire trove of coupons.

When you're using coupons at the store, pay attention to them to ensure that they're scanning as they should. You would be surprised at how many coupons do not scan at the register, whether it be a problem with a coupon or with the store. Carefully watch your cashier scan your coupons and watch the screen to make sure they went through.

Try to match your coupons to the stores sale ads. This will give you the most bang for your buck. A lot of coupons don't expire for at least three months, so keep your coupons handy for a sale. You might be able to save an insane amount of money if you stack coupons with in store sales.

Signing up for a couponing website is a good idea so that you can trade with people from other areas. Many companies will print coupons in one area of the country that they do not in others. They are still good nationally, but they may just not be available to you.

For someone who is really into clipping coupons, there are sites online that will let you purchase coupons. You might even find a deal on coupons that give you free things. If you can get multiple for a small amount of money, it could result in steep savings later.

Cut grocery coupons from the newspaper. Most Sunday papers distributed by major newspapers include a coupon section. If you don't get the newspaper, you can buy one from a newsstand. There are also vending machines outside many retail establishments. Even if you don't read the newspaper, the Sunday paper is a wise investment for coupon shoppers.

Try contacting the manufacturer directly. If there is a product that you love, but don't often find coupons for, try contacting the company directly. Express your enthusiasm for their products and ask if they have any coupons available. Who knows? You may score some great deals on a brand you really love!

Use rewards coupons carefully. You will very rarely get coupons for certain items, like milk or meats. Some stores offer rewards coupons and certificates for certain purchases, and these can be used for anything in the store. Take advantage of them and use them on products like milk, fruits and veggies, or meats.

Match your coupons up with sale items. Once you get the ad for the grocery store's weekly sale, find items to buy that you use and have coupons for. Using a coupon on a sale item saves you even more money than just using the coupon on a regular priced item.

To make your coupon hobby run more smoothly, try purchasing a three-ring binder, and fill it with baseball card collector sheets. Each sheet contains 9 pockets that you can fill with your coupons. Coupons can then be divided into categories, such as cleaning supplies, beauty products and many other categories.

Look for retailers that accept double coupons. You will save twice as much on that item if it is a double coupon. This can prove convenient for pricier items that only have coupons in small amounts, like paper towels. Carefully check out your coupons because some will actually say they do not double, which means this doubling option doesn't apply for them.

Go online. There are a lot of coupons on the Internet that aren't available in your local papers.

Not only that, but some companies offer Internet only deals that others are not going to get. Before you buy anything, check online and do a search to find any coupons available.

Put your scissors down! Instead of spending time clipping coupons that you may or may not ever use, just keep the whole circular. Organize them in a file chronologically. There are many blogs and databases online that will match up coupons with in-store sales and refer you to the dated insert with the corresponding coupon. When you find a deal you want, just look up the inserts and clip only the coupons you'll need.

When you go shopping, leave the children at home. Children will get you off your shopping and coupon list and try to get you to buy impulse items for them. They are a distraction and difficult to keep entertained while shopping. If you can leave them at home with your partner, that is your best choice.

Set a time during the week to clip out coupons to save money. You have to put in a little time if you really want to save money with coupons. If you are going to take it seriously, schedule time for it. Allot at least 30 minutes per day to look for and cut out coupons.

To make the most from coupons, you should make sure you have a subscription to your local Sunday paper. There are coupons in the newspaper every day of the week. However, the sheer volume and variety of coupons in the Sunday paper will more than offset the cost of the subscription.

To know where you can use certain coupons, write down a list of the coupon policies at your local retailers and grocers. Some of them are not going to accept the Internet printed coupons, or competitors. Check their websites for their policies, and consider trips to stores you might not currently visit if they are more coupons friendly.

Save smarter by only using coupons for things you were going to buy anyway. Lots of people end up paying good money for items they really have no use for. Unless it's something, you know you and your family will make good use of, don't just get something because you have a great coupon for it.

Many stores have an online store, and you can sign up for notifications when they have a sale. You can also check the site for current coupon offers periodically. You can print the coupon from their website, or use the code they provide if you want to order an item online.

Look online for your favorite coupons before going shopping. Many stores offer coupons on their websites, and there are also sites dedicated strictly to coupons. You can find them for almost every different type of item, and they often offer substantial savings, sometimes even on items that are already on sale.

Print coupons from the Internet. There are many websites that offer manufacturers coupons for you to print and use at many different stores. Sometimes the manufacturer's website even has printable coupons you can use. Different stores have different policies regarding printed coupons so be sure to check your store's policy.

Know which stores near you offer the lowest price to begin with, then go to them with your coupons. If store X is selling an item at two dollars more than most and your coupon is for a dollar off, you are just selling yourself short! Do the basic legwork and maximize your total savings!

A good tip you can try out if you're into using coupons is to subscribe to the newsletter of all your favorite stores. This is a win-win scenario because the store is holding onto you as a consumer, and they in turn will provide you with special coupons that you can use.

Take the hassle out of using coupons by staying organized. If your coupons are flying all about your purse, it's enough to stress you out. Buy a coupon organizer and use it. Coupon organizers have tabs so that you can separate coupons by category. If you don't want to buy one, you can make one yourself.

To maximize your coupons from savings, take the time to check the prices on all the options when you shop. For example, if you have a coupon for $1 off a bottle of Windex, but the store brand glass cleaner is $2 cheaper than the price of Windex, then you'll be ahead without the coupon.

Keep your eye out for coupons in unexpected places. The phone book, the backs of receipts, and newspapers are great places to find these tickets to savings. The coupons in these locations are often for restaurants, mechanics, salons and other experiences or services. There's no reason to limit your coupon usage to grocery shopping!

Save twice as much money by stacking store coupons with manufacturer's coupons. This is the best way to get the most money off when couponing. Look at the weekly ad circular's to see what's on sale, then go to the manufacturer's site and see if they have a coupon. This way, you can "double-up" and save the most money!

To keep from wasting your coupons, go through the ones you've clipped out at least twice a month. That way you can clean out the ones that have expired and remember the offers you have, so that when you go to the store, your coupons will go with you.

Now that you've read all these tips, you can see how easy it is to save money by using coupons. Whether you find them online, or cut them out of newspapers, coupons can be a great cash-saving tool. Implement what you've just learned, and watch your monthly budget stretch before your eyes.

Looking For Some Coupon Tips? You've Come To The Right Place

By utilizing coupons, you can save some cash. After you read and apply what you learn here, compare your grocery will with a friend's. Coupons can help you to cut costs greatly. You may be surprised. Continue on with this post to learn some great tips for coupon collecting.

Look for ways to double up sales with coupons. In many cases, it's a better idea to hold onto your coupons for a week or two instead of making use of them immediately. You may also need to go to multiple stores when shopping to see the savings that you want to see.

To maximize your savings when using coupons, use them to purchase items that are on sale and at supermarkets that offer double or triple coupon savings. When you buy an item that is on sale and use a coupon that is doubled or tripled, you may find that you pay pennies for the item or even get it for free!

A good tip when clipping out coupons is to place them in a pouch or somewhere you can easily keep track of them. This will prevent you from creating a mess and you'll have your coupons readily available when you need them so you won't have to dig around to find them.

Set one day each week to go "couponing." This will help you become more efficient. There's nothing stopping you from clipping a coupon right when it catches your eye, but making a concentrated effort once a week to pore over newspapers and websites will allow you to plan out plenty of great discount shopping trips for the coming week.

Make sure you understand and print off coupon policies for your local stores. Walmart, for example, has a printable coupon policy. Keep them in your coupon organizer for handy usage. On occasion, a cashier may not know the corporate policies for their stores, and having the policy may help you get the leg up in a disagreement.

Go through the ads before clipping coupons so you can find coupons for things you plan to buy. You may find that visiting a couple of stores can help you save a ton of money.

Whenever you go shopping, make a budget and stick to it. If you are using coupons to save money, you have to stick to your food budget and keep your money in your pocket, not on impulse spending. If you have extra money after shopping, put it aside so that you can stock up on something special another week.

Cut grocery coupons from the newspaper. Most

Sunday papers distributed by major newspapers include a coupon section. If you don't get the newspaper, you can buy one from a newsstand. There are also vending machines outside many retail establishments. Even if you don't read the newspaper, the Sunday paper is a wise investment for coupon shoppers.

A helpful tip for couponers is to organize and store your coupons where they can be found easily when you are ready to shop. Sometimes people do not remember their coupons when they go shopping, so keep them in plain sight so you will not forget them.

When using your coupons, try to find stores that will double or triple them. Some stores do this on a regular basis, while others offer special offers for a particular week or weekend. By doing this, you can save twice as much on your purchases. Just keep your eye on the local newspapers to find out who is offering doubles or triples and when.

To make sure you can use your coupons when the time comes, never leave them laying out in sunlight. Coupons laid on a counter or table near a window, or even worse-on a car dashboard, are going to receive a lot of radiation that discolors them. When the time comes to use them, they may be so faded that they are refused.

To make your coupon hobby run more smoothly, try purchasing a three-ring binder, and fill it with baseball card collector sheets. Each sheet contains 9 pockets that you can fill with your coupons. Coupons can then be divided into categories, such as cleaning supplies, beauty products and many other categories.

Do you have more than one of the same coupon? You can usually use more than one coupon at the same time. Just make sure you follow the rules on the coupon and buy the amount of product that your coupons are for. For instance, if you have four coupons for one item, you can buy four items.

It is important to have your coupons organized, to avoid expiration dates passing without your knowledge. In addition to sorting by type, put the ones with the soonest expiration dates first. When you see that the time is approaching, add the item to your shopping list. Knowing what you have in advance will also help you to work with the in-store sales.

Share the information you have learned about saving money with coupons with others. By sharing information, you will get information back. You will also meet other people who are collecting coupons and might be willing to trade with you. This is a great way to help everyone save more money in a tight economy.

Try to remember that couponing is not free. You do have to invest your time and organization into the ordeal. Also, never just buy something because you have a coupon. Stay within your budget. If you spend money just because you feel like you are saving money, you are in fact wasting money.

Try to find websites that showcase your manufacturers for the best deals. Consider companies you can always bank on, like Stouffers. You should register your email address on their websites so that you can obtain significant savings that can't be found on coupon roundup sites. They love to reward special customers with great coupon deals.

If you are going to make the most out of your coupons, make sure you are well aware of what policy is in place at the store you wish to redeem them at. Some stores, for example, have a limit on the number of coupons or which ones they will accept.

If you want to get the most of your couponing endeavors, check out some websites that are dedicated to helping you save big. From sites that offer to send you coupons for a small fee to those that send out coupons for free or tell you where to find them, there is no shortage of coupon websites out there.

You'll find great coupons in newspapers, so make sure you're subscribing to several of them. This is especially true of the Sunday paper. Don't just get one copy. Buy several copies. More often than not, you will find that you are saving far more than what you spent on the newspapers.

Keep all your coupons in one place. Some coupons are really small, and you don't want to lose them. You also don't want to have coupons all over the house. When you keep them all in one place, you can locate them when you need them without too much trouble.

Don't only use one newspaper. Subscribe to multiple ones for weekend delivery, or you can ask your friends or family for the copies after they are done. The more newspapers you have, the more coupons you have to choose from. Even those duplicate coupons will come in handy when you shop on different days.

Shop at stores that multiply coupons. Some stores double or triple coupons everyday. Other stores have certain days on which they will multiply manufacturer coupons. Be sure to read the fine print, because some stores just allow a limited number to be multiplied, require a minimum purchase, or only multiply coupons with lower values.

Join like-minded people on forums and social networks to really empower your couponing. Few things are loved by more people and with such passion as saving money, so find a site where people share their tips, codes and strategies to saving more money with the use of money saving coupons.

A good way to save money through coupons is by using their loyalty or rewards program. A lot of times stores will offer incentives for you to continue shopping there so they will offer you points. After getting enough of these points, the amount can be applied towards your next purchase.

Compare prices between the warehouse and the grocer. There can often be a better deal waiting for you at the your local 'warehouse' store. Check online or check the prices between the two, in person, and evaluate the best use of your coupons. You may buy a little more, yet save a little more as well.

Ask your family and friends to not throw away the coupons that come with their Sunday paper or magazines. This will provide you with more resources for your coupons, especially for items you want to stock up on. In order to encourage their support, consider giving back by offering up items you are able to purchase with the coupons.

Before beginning any couponing strategy, review your budget and spending habits. Do you spend more at the grocery store than you can afford? Make a log that tracks how prices fluctuate weekly and when stores offer in-store coupons. By making a log of this information, you can effectively save at least one-quarter of your grocery budget.

Look at coupons the same way you look at cash.

Many people do not realize that each coupon used results in actual money in their pocket. For example, a twenty-five cent coupon does not seem like much, but when you start viewing coupons as actual money you will realize that those twenty-five cent coupons add up quickly to dollars.

A good tip if you're someone that uses coupons is to use a coupon on an item that you'd like to try out. Sometimes we'd like to try out new products but don't want to pay full price for them. Using a coupon will sweeten the deal, and you'll get a chance to try out the product for yourself.

Do not make the mistake of not using as many coupons as you can to get discounts. For example, if you have four bags of chips, and you have a coupon for a discount on one bag, you can get three more coupons and get a discount off of everyone.

Sign up for the mailing lists of your favorite stores and brands. Many companies send out coupons to people subscribed to their list that aren't available otherwise. Stores also send valuable store-specific coupons like a percentage of your purchase or a dollar amount off a purchase of a certain amount.

Use a system for keeping your coupons tidy and

organized. Envelopes, binders or expandable files are all great tools. Not only, being organized keep you from forgetting to use your coupons, but it saves time at the register. Preparing ahead of time keeps you from having to dig for and sort coupons while checking out, leading to quick grocery trips.

A great tip for anyone who uses coupons regularly is to keep them organized. Try keeping them in a binder and arrange them in a way that makes sense to you so that you will be able to find any coupon you need at any time with very little effort.

When you plan on being an extreme coupon clipper you must make sure you know exactly what the rules and policies are at your favorite store. There may be one store that will double coupons and another one of the stores that you frequent that do not double the coupons.

You can find coupons in lots of different places. An old-fashioned favorite is the Sunday paper. You can also find coupons in coupon mailings, grocery store fliers, and magazines. There are numerous coupon and discount websites where coupons and promotion codes can be found.

Another method of getting coupons is to stop by

your local cafe on Sunday. Many coffee shops provide their customers with free newspapers, and will often hand over the coupons to the first person who asks. Do not be afraid to ask for what you need! People are often willing to help out.

Familiarize yourself with coupon terminology. You don't want to get to the front register and find out you can't use half your coupons. Look at your coupons before you make the trip to the store. Make sure you're reading the fine print. Make sure you understand the jargon that is used on it.

Acquire copies of the couponing policies at the stores you frequent, and keep them in your coupon binder on each shopping trip. Having this policies in writing can help to clear up any misunderstandings at the register quickly. Many stores make their policies regarding coupons available on their web sites.

Go ahead and get the Sunday paper so that you can find all of the coupons and discounts that are in them. You can save a lot of money buy paying a few dollars to purchase the Sunday paper for all of the coupons that are inside of it that offer you good deals.

In some stores you can double up or even triple up your coupons. If you happen to be a coupon novice, just make a few inquiries about which local stores offer such deals. Your neighbors and co-workers can lead you into the right locations.

Cut grocery coupons from the newspaper. Most Sunday papers distributed by major newspapers include a coupon section. If you don't get the newspaper, you can buy one from a newsstand. There are also vending machines outside many retail establishments. Even if you don't read the newspaper, the Sunday paper is a wise investment for coupon shoppers.

Understand grocery pricing in general. You may think that getting a coupon means you are getting great savings, but sometimes that isn't the case. Know what the price of the item is in the first place, and keep an eye on price-comparison websites that can give you a general idea of what the products are really worth.

If your Sunday paper has a great coupon circular, buy more than one copy. The cost of the paper is often less than the savings the coupons offer if they are for items or brands that your family regularly uses. In addition to buying extra copies, you can also ask your friends or family members for their copies.

Learn what the regular prices are for items that you use frequently, or for expensive items that you only purchase occasionally. Sometimes, stores will raise the prices of items before putting them on sale or offering other in store specials. By learning the true regular price, you are prepared for these events.

When using coupons, it is important to recognize that small amounts of money add up over time into large amounts. Coupon savings of only 10 or 25 cents may not seem like very much, but you would be surprised at just how much money these small value coupons will end up saving you over your life time. Save little to save big.

Make sure that you are aware of all the regulations for using the coupons that you have. Sometimes, you are not able to double up on coupons for the same item, or you may find yourself in a situation where a store will only accept a maximum amount of coupons for a particular purchase.

Try to remember that couponing is not free. You do have to invest your time and organization into the ordeal. Also, never just buy something because you have a coupon. Stay within your budget. If you spend money just because you feel like you are saving money, you are in fact wasting money.

Keep your eye out for coupons in unexpected places. The phone book, the backs of receipts, and newspapers are great places to find these tickets to savings. The coupons in these locations are often for restaurants, mechanics, salons and other experiences or services. There's no reason to limit your coupon usage to grocery shopping!

Take advantage of coupons and use them to save on products that you intend to actually use. Many people buy things just because there is a coupon for them and they end up not using them. This defeats the purpose of a coupon since you will end up wasting money when you throw these items away.

Signing up for online coupon websites is a great way to get coupons without having to buy a newspaper. You can customize your profile on the website so that you are sent coupons that are of most interest to you. Often, there will be special coupons and deals that are only given to people who are members of these websites.

Another method of getting coupons is to stop by your local cafe on Sunday. Many coffee shops provide their customers with free newspapers, and will often hand over the coupons to the first person who asks. Do not be afraid to ask for what you need! People are often willing to help out.

Go online. There are a lot of coupons on the Internet that aren't available in your local papers. Not only that, but some companies offer Internet only deals that others are not going to get. Before you buy anything, check online and do a search to find any coupons available.

It is a good idea to have a large coupon holder and organizer. This way when you are clipping coupons, you will be organized and know exactly where to look for it. If it is large, you will have plenty of room to clip all the coupons you find and possibly trade them with others.

To truly maximize your coupon benefits, you should learn coupon jargon. These are words that you will see on various coupons. Some popular coupon terms are "BOGO," "MIR," and "OYNO." These terms mean, "Buy One Get One," "Mail-In Rebate," and "On Your Next Order." Taking the time to learn these terms and many more can really boost your savings.

Use rewards coupons carefully. You will very rarely get coupons for certain items, like milk or meats. Some stores offer rewards coupons and certificates for certain purchases, and these can be used for anything in the store. Take advantage of them and use them on products like milk, fruits and veggies, or meats.

If you snag a truly great deal with a coupon for an item that you won't use, donate it. Food banks will accept nearly any packaged food item. Women's shelters can often use diapers, shampoo, and other toiletries and supplies. Research and contact local resources in your community to find out what they need, and use your couponing skills for good.

A good coupon tip you should use is to do all of your shopping at the end of the month. Most stores have it so that their coupons expire at the end of the month. Shopping during this time will make it more convenient for you to get the best deals.

You can really save a lot of money when you have coupons that get you up to 75% off the retail price. When you encounter coupons like this, you should stock up on the items for at least a three-month supply. This also gives you time to look for additional coupons during that time period to help you replenish your stock when it is low.

Having brand loyalty is not always wise if you are going to be using coupons for savings. For instance, you may enjoy Pepsi, but if Coca Cola is the brand that is on sale and you have coupons for it, that is what you should go with. Being faithful to a brand is not going to save you money.

Do not forget the internet for coupons. There are hundreds of websites that will have coupons listed on them that are available to print for free. These coupons are totally legitimate, but you have to make sure that your store will accept them. There is some coupon fraud in the world and some stores will no longer accept internet printed coupons.

Find out how much others are saving with coupons. The reason you want to do this is because you will find that the stories from other people can inspire you and motivate you to stick your coupon regiment. Hearing that people saved money makes you feel more likely to do the same!

Buy in bulks. This is one of the most cost-effective

ways to use coupons. Collect several coupons of the items you use frequently and look for sales to match your coupons. For example, if your family uses a lot of tomato sauce, collect those coupons and wait for the item to go on sale and then purchase as many of the items as you have coupons.

Have your kids help you, and implement that child labor law within the household. If your kids pitch in, you can make coupon hunting much faster. At the same time, it helps them learn knowledgeable skills about cutting costs when it comes to shopping for groceries. Teach them, and help yourself.

Let brand-name manufacturers collect your personal data. Sure, you might get a bunch of junk mail you have to throw out, but all those exclusive coupons you get will save you so much money, you won't care! Fill out coupon surveys and watch for those amazing coupons to start arriving in your mailbox.

Get your kids involved in clipping coupons by offering them a portion of the money, they help you save. If a child locates $10 worth of coupons for products that your family uses, give her a portion of the money for her savings account or piggy bank.

This is a great way to explain budgeting, saving and other financial principles.

Take advantage of coupons and use them to save on products that you intend to actually use. Many people buy things just because there is a coupon for them and they end up not using them. This defeats the purpose of a coupon since you will end up wasting money when you throw these items away.

When you have a manufacturer's coupon, you can stack that coupon with store coupons. This is a great way to get items for next to free or almost free. Use the store's coupons from their weekly circular and match them up with coupons from the manufacturer off the Internet or from the newspaper.

If you are into couponing, chances are you have some friends and family who are not; so, to save even more money, ask them for spare coupons. Often, companies mail out great high-value coupons or include them in inserts in the local newspaper. Ask friends and family to set them aside for you if they won't be using them.

If you carry a loyalty card for a particular store, check the store's website for coupons. Many retailers offer manufacturer's coupons on their website and allow you to download them to your card. Your stored coupons are automatically deducted when the cashier swipes your card at the cash register.

Look for coupons before purchasing items online. This is very easy to do. Fire up your internet, open your browser, and just type in the product's name followed by "coupon." Your search results should give you current coupon codes. You can find a wide range of coupons out there, from initial savings on the purchase to free shipping coupon codes to use at checkout.

A good way to save money through coupons is by using their loyalty or rewards program. A lot of times stores will offer incentives for you to continue shopping there so they will offer you points. After getting enough of these points, the amount can be applied towards your next purchase.

Understand grocery pricing in general. You may think that getting a coupon means you are getting great savings, but sometimes that isn't the case. Know what the price of the item is in the first place, and keep an eye on price-comparison websites that can give you a general idea of what the products are really worth.

If you snag a truly great deal with a coupon for an item that you won't use, donate it. Food banks will accept nearly any packaged food item. Women's shelters can often use diapers, shampoo, and other toiletries and supplies. Research and contact local resources in your community to find out what they need, and use your couponing skills for good.

Target the smaller sizes on the grocery shelf to maximize your coupon. The reduction in size also carries a reduction in initial price. When you reduce your unit cost, you save more in the long run. This will let you control your usage of products better overall as well.

The best coupon websites will give you a list of all of the major stores and tell you where you can find the best coupons to go with their weekly deals. You need to pay attention to these and do not forget about your chain drug stores that always have good coupon deals.

Match your coupons up with sale items. Once you get the ad for the grocery store's weekly sale, find items to buy that you use and have coupons for.

Using a coupon on a sale item saves you even more money than just using the coupon on a regular priced item.

To make finding your coupons easier, try sorting them by a similar attribute. For instance, you could sort them by brand, by product type, by expiration date, etc. There are so many ways you can keep everything together so that you can easily see and use them to maximize your savings.

Before beginning any couponing strategy, review your budget and spending habits. Do you spend more at the grocery store than you can afford? Make a log that tracks how prices fluctuate weekly and when stores offer in-store coupons. By making a log of this information, you can effectively save at least one-quarter of your grocery budget.

Instead of spending a large amount of money buying newspapers, enlist the help of your neighbors, friends and co-workers. Ask anyone who doesn't use their Sunday coupon inserts to save them for you. It's the perfect method for receiving free coupons. In return you can give them free goods as a reward.

Search the weekly ad's and circulars for items that

are on sale. You can then search for coupons for those items and get the best deal possible. You can find coupons online at a coupon website, on eBay, on the manufacturers' website and in the newspaper. Combine these coupons with the sales to get the best price

Find out how much others are saving with coupons. The reason you want to do this is because you will find that the stories from other people can inspire you and motivate you to stick your coupon regiment. Hearing that people saved money makes you feel more likely to do the same!

Get a store saving's card for every place you shop. Holders of these cards get exclusive savings and bonuses, even without picking up a pair of scissors or warming up the printer. If you don't like the store tracking your data, just put false information on the application when you sign-up, and you can maintain complete anonymity.

Check out your favorite manufacturers' websites in order to locate opportunities for great coupons. Proctor and Gamble is a great site to use for deals on the most widely used products. To receive extra savings, you can get some great deals by submitting your email to sign up for specials. Subscribing to a website can wind up saving you a lot in the future.

Various options exist for locating coupons. An old-fashioned favorite is the Sunday paper. Also, find them in grocery store circulars, magazines and coupon mailings. You can even find lots of online sites that will let you pick and choose coupons to print out.

Another method of getting coupons is to stop by your local cafe on Sunday. Many coffee shops provide their customers with free newspapers, and will often hand over the coupons to the first person who asks. Do not be afraid to ask for what you need! People are often willing to help out.

Shop at local stores that honor competitor's coupons to minimize your shopping trips. If you find that your neighborhood store will accept the competitor coupons and perhaps even double them, you have found your go to store!

It is a good idea to have a large coupon holder and organizer. This way when you are clipping coupons, you will be organized and know exactly where to look for it. If it is large, you will have plenty of room to clip all the coupons you find and possibly trade them with others.

A great tip when using coupons is to keep track of the expiration date. You don't want to walk into a store, pick up an item and then present the cashier with a coupon that's expired. Some stores might still honor the deal but most won't, and you'll be embarrassed.

Shop weekly to best utilize your coupons. Even if all you get are the weekly specials, shopping weekly is worth it. Most stores offer weekly coupons that will allow you to maximize your coupon savings.

One key tip for anyone who collects coupons is to never throw away those coupons you get in the mail. You can actually get some great value in these coupons, particularly with fast-food restaurants. Make sure that you at least glance over them before throwing anything away in the garbage.

Many stores have an online store, and you can sign up for notifications when they have a sale. You can also check the site for current coupon offers periodically. You can print the coupon from their website, or use the code they provide if you want to order an item online.

Try to stack your coupons. Sometimes stores will allow you to use both a manufacturer's coupon and a store coupon for one item. Professional couponers find that this often leads to items that cost only pennies, or are at times even free. Always ask if you can stack coupons when you are at the checkout stand to save the most money.

Keep your coupons organized. Whether you use a coupon holder, binder or envelopes, make sure your coupons are organized and easy to find. Organize them in a way that is easiest for you to sort through. Some ideas are sorting by item type or the section of the store the item is kept in.

Those of you who are bargain shoppers and who love to use coupons to save would be wise to browse through a store's clearance section. The savings you can get with a clearance item coupled with a coupon can be quite significant. Make sure to see if any items on clearance are still eligible for coupon use.

Only purchase what you have room for. Coupons for perishable items that you probably won't use are best given to a friend and not used yourself.

Stop spending the full amount on things that you

buy. All it takes is five minutes to look up if there are any coupons online, and by doing this you can save a bunch of money whenever you buy anything. Look in magazines, online, or through articles to find coupons.

It is important to have your coupons with you whenever you are out shopping. If your coupons are at home in a drawer waiting for a shopping trip, then you will miss great deals when you shop on the spur of the moment. Keep them in your glove compartment or handbag so you can pull them out at any time.

Understand that you may need to alter your shopping list for the sake of using your coupons. Buy lots of an item that is non-perishable when you have the coupons available. That will produce great long-term savings.

Do what it takes to break anyone in your household of brand loyalty. Being emotionally attached to one particular brand of any product is going to really restrict your couponing opportunities on that kind of item. You need to be flexible and willing to stock up on months' worth of a name or alternate brand when the deal strikes.

Get your kids involved in clipping coupons by offering them a portion of the money, they help you save. If a child locates $10 worth of coupons for products that your family uses, give her a portion of the money for her savings account or piggy bank. This is a great way to explain budgeting, saving and other financial principles.

Recruit your friends in couponing so you can trade coupons with each other to maximize the deals. If you have a coupon that they need, but which you do not, you can be a help to them. If you have a lot of friends, you can create a coupon swap day every month. You will also get together with friends and chat.

Only use coupons for products that you will actually use. You won't save any money by purchasing items that your family does not need or brands that you don't like just because you have a coupon. Cutting out coupons for items you don't use also costs you time, which could be better spent.

Use a search engine to find discounts or coupons for online retailers you customarily patronize. The codes are sometimes valid for percentage discounts, free shipping, or other promotional offers.

Start by subscribing to newsletters that will offer you discounts from time to time. When you do this, you can find a lot of coupons from being emailed by different websites. You don't have to use them whenever you get them, but if you find a deal, then you could be in luck.

Store your coupons in little plastic baggies. This will save you time when you're looking for one in particular, and they keep them looking neat. They won't go flying all around the place, and they won't get wet. Storing coupons in these little bags makes sense and will help you save.

To get additional newspaper coupon inserts, contact your local paper's office and inquire about couponer discounts. A lot of local papers will give you a discount if you order multiple copies each week.

Do not buy something just because you have a coupon for it. Many extreme couponers will only buy an item because they have a coupon for it; this can make you waste tons of money. Instead, hold onto the coupon and when the item is on sale, use it then.

Join like-minded people on forums and social networks to really empower your couponing. Few things are loved by more people and with such passion as saving money, so find a site where people share their tips, codes and strategies to saving more money with the use of money saving coupons.

Understand grocery pricing in general. You may think that getting a coupon means you are getting great savings, but sometimes that isn't the case. Know what the price of the item is in the first place, and keep an eye on price-comparison websites that can give you a general idea of what the products are really worth.

To get the most coupons possible, sign up for more than one Sunday newspaper subscription. You will receive tons of coupons this way and may even get different ones with each subscriptions. Also, ask your family and friends to save the coupons from their papers for you (if they are not using them).

If you like a product, look on the package and see if there is a 1-800 number you can call. Often these numbers are used for complaints, but you can call them and they might send you coupons. If you want to search on Facebook as well, many companies offer coupons for their Facebook subscribers only.

Try to find some of the sites online that will offer the best coupons in the stores that you shop in your area. This will give you the ability to get the most out of the coupons that you purchase and maximize the savings that you will have in the long run.

A great way to save money with coupons is by not limiting yourself to just the larger items. Even the smaller 25 cent coupons will add up over time, and you will end up saving a lot more money on a yearly basis. So start stocking up and saving money!

If a product has a mail-in rebate offer, make sure that it is worth the postage and your time. If it is, make certain that you mail it in quickly. Some stores will offer you a special receipt, specifically for rebates. If your store doesn't, pay for the item separately so that you have your receipt for other items.

There are a lot of coupons you can get by joining a company's social media website. Search for their business name and then follow them. A lot of places offer coupons regularly, for contests or even just for joining their site. Social media is very popular now, so it shouldn't be hard to locate your favorite companies. You may even get free samples!

Only use coupons on items that are on sale. You can get the most out of your money this way. If an item is not on sale and you buy it just because you have a coupon, you could be wasting money. Hold on to your coupons until the next week when sales change and the item you want is on sale.

To minimize conflicts when you go shopping, keep a hard copy of the store coupon policy in your coupon binder. This way, if a cashier or manager says that your coupons can not be combined, you have the store words to back you up. You may choose to review the policy beforehand, to ensure you understand it.

If you are couponing to save on groceries, remember that you can't favor brands. You have to be willing to purchase items that are both on sale and that you have coupons for. While it may be okay to keep one or two favorites, in general, you have to be flexible.

Try to remember that couponing is not free. You do have to invest your time and organization into the ordeal. Also, never just buy something because you have a coupon. Stay within your budget. If you spend money just because you feel like you are saving money, you are in fact wasting money.

When you have a manufacturer's coupon, you can stack that coupon with store coupons. This is a great way to get items for next to free or almost free. Use the store's coupons from their weekly circular and match them up with coupons from the manufacturer off the Internet or from the newspaper.

Use coupons when items go on sale. In many cases, it's a better idea to hold onto your coupons for a week or two instead of making use of them immediately. However, the savings will be worth the wait.

Keep all your coupons in one place. Some coupons are really small, and you don't want to lose them. You also don't want to have coupons all over the house. When you keep them all in one place, you can locate them when you need them without too much trouble.

It is a good idea to have a large coupon holder and organizer. This way when you are clipping coupons, you will be organized and know exactly where to look for it. If it is large, you will have plenty of room to clip all the coupons you find and possibly trade them with others.

A good tip when clipping out coupons is to place them in a pouch or somewhere you can easily keep track of them. This will prevent you from creating a mess and you'll have your coupons readily available when you need them so you won't have to dig around to find them.

Request all the free sample offers you can find. Not only will you get the free sample in the mail, but often times you'll receive a coupon for the item as well. Coupons that come with free samples tend to be higher value than others, so you'll get a great sample and a great deal!

Take your time. You don't have to be a couponing expert overnight. Begin by frequenting just one store. Get used to its policies and figure out how best to manage your coupons. Once you start to get the hang of things, pick up a second store. Eventually, you may have several that you visit on a regular basis.

Go ahead and get the Sunday paper so that you can find all of the coupons and discounts that are in them. You can save a lot of money buy paying a few dollars to purchase the Sunday paper for all of the coupons that are inside of it that offer you good deals.

Join like-minded people on forums and social networks to really empower your couponing. Few things are loved by more people and with such passion as saving money, so find a site where people share their tips, codes and strategies to saving more money with the use of money saving coupons.

If your Sunday paper has a great coupon circular, buy more than one copy. The cost of the paper is often less than the savings the coupons offer if they are for items or brands that your family regularly uses. In addition to buying extra copies, you can also ask your friends or family members for their copies.

Keep your eyes peeled for peelies! When wandering through your local store, be on the lookout for coupons stuck to the outside of products or hanging around the necks of bottles. These are called peelies and hangtags in coupon lingo, and can save you big bucks! Also look for coupon dispensers in aisles to save even more.

Start your coupon collecting with only one store. Coupons may seem like an easy thing to collect and utilize, but there are many complexities. Some coupons have multiple policies. Some stores allow coupons from competitors. Some stores will even accept coupons that have expired - even months after the expiration date.

You may know to subscribe to the Sunday paper; however, you should also subscribe to magazines that offer coupons. Check online for circulars that are popular within the couponing community. Often, these magazines will have garnered great coupons that are hard to find, if not impossible to find, anywhere else.

You can even find coupons and special promotional discounts for services online. A lot of rental car agencies will allow you to use a coupon or promotional code to get a discount for their services. Just do a quick search to see what you can find and you can wind up saving a good amount of money.

For the best in grocery coupon info, visit your local store's site first! Many people don't realize that their favorite grocery store has a homepage filled with amazing enticements, and they generally stick with coupon and manufacturer sites. Bookmark your neighborhood store and sign up for more savings with email alerts!

Organizing your coupons is the best way to make the most of them. many of the most successful couponers use a binder with clear plastic pages that are sold to store collector cards in. These will help you to easily see all of your coupons easily and to organize them in categories.

Signing up for online coupon websites is a great way to get coupons without having to buy a newspaper. You can customize your profile on the website so that you are sent coupons that are of most interest to you. Often, there will be special coupons and deals that are only given to people who are members of these websites.

To get coupons for brands you particularly enjoy, all you have to do is ask. Many companies are willing to send out coupons to people who email or write to them. Simply send a letter noting how much you enjoy a product and ask if they would provide you with coupons. You will be surprised at how often they oblige!

Go online. There are a lot of coupons on the Internet that aren't available in your local papers. Not only that, but some companies offer Internet only deals that others are not going to get. Before you buy anything, check online and do a search to find any coupons available.

Familiarize yourself with coupon terminology. You don't want to get to the front register and find out you can't use half your coupons. Look at your coupons before you make the trip to the store. Make sure you're reading the fine print. Make sure you understand the jargon that is used on it.

Many stores let you double, and sometimes even triple coupons. All you have to do is ask the stores to see if they will let you stack coupons. You can also ask others what type of experience they have had using coupons in different locations.

Keep your eyes peeled for peelies! When wandering through your local store, be on the lookout for coupons stuck to the outside of products or hanging around the necks of bottles. These are called peelies and hangtags in coupon lingo, and can save you big bucks! Also look for coupon dispensers in aisles to save even more.

If a product has a mail-in rebate offer, make sure that it is worth the postage and your time. If it is, make certain that you mail it in quickly. Some stores will offer you a special receipt, specifically for rebates. If your store doesn't, pay for the item separately so that you have your receipt for other items.

Always be respectful when using your coupons. Be sure that you get items that you're going to use and also make sure that your coupons are not expired. A lot of stores adjust policies about coupons if too many folks do that, and that means less savings all around.

Print coupons from the Internet. There are many websites that offer manufacturers coupons for you to print and use at many different stores. Sometimes the manufacturer's website even has printable coupons you can use. Different stores have different policies regarding printed coupons so be sure to check your store's policy.

If you are couponing to save on groceries, remember that you can't favor brands. You have to be willing to purchase items that are both on sale and that you have coupons for. While it may be okay to keep one or two favorites, in general, you have to be flexible.

Keep in mind that some places will not allow you to stack discounts on one another. You are most likely going to have to choose one or the other if you are trying to use a coupon on an item that is on sale, so choose the cheapest of the two prices.

Buy in bulks. This is one of the most cost-effective ways to use coupons. Collect several coupons of the items you use frequently and look for sales to match your coupons. For example, if your family uses a lot of tomato sauce, collect those coupons and wait for the item to go on sale and then purchase as many of the items as you have coupons.

If you enter a store with a lot of coupons, be polite to the cashiers and the managers. Your massive amount of coupons are going to be a headache to them as well as the customers behind you in line. You need these people to be on your side to make the experience a positive one.

Get a store saving's card for every place you shop. Holders of these cards get exclusive savings and bonuses, even without picking up a pair of scissors or warming up the printer. If you don't like the store tracking your data, just put false information on the application when you sign-up, and you can maintain complete anonymity.

Create your shopping list before you go to the store based on the coupons you want to use. You can also use the coupons you have to get ideas on what meals to cook that week. This will help you save time while shopping and make sure you use the coupons you have instead of letting them expire.

Join a rewards program at the store you go to if they have one. Most of the time, you'll be able to get coupons in the mail or access them online. You usually get a card, and will be able to rack up discounts, as well as get discounts on everyday items.

Many successful coupon users have many friends who also use coupons, and they often trade out coupons they don't need for coupons that they do need. Not everyone uses the same products so having a coupon buddy can be a great way to get the coupons that are of most use to you.

Organize your coupons. You can purchase coupon organizers and binders at many mass retail chains as well as online stores. You can organize your coupons by subject, or by the expiration date. Each compartment or sleeve can be labeled with the information you need. Another inexpensive option is to place coupons in separate envelopes.

To help you get the most out of your coupon usage, you should strive to only use coupons on items that you actually use. Oftentimes people cut out the coupons and end up buying things they do not need. This ends up in you overspending on items that you would never have bought.

If you want to get the most of your couponing endeavors, check out some websites that are dedicated to helping you save big. From sites that offer to send you coupons for a small fee to those that send out coupons for free or tell you where to find them, there is no shortage of coupon websites out there.

It is a good idea to have a large coupon holder and organizer. This way when you are clipping coupons, you will be organized and know exactly where to look for it. If it is large, you will have plenty of room to clip all the coupons you find and possibly trade them with others.

Look at your list before you go to the grocery store. Check over the items you need and see if there are any coupons available online. You can also check the flyer from the store you visit most often to see if any of the items you need are on sale.

When grocery shopping with a lot of coupons, don't visit the store at peak hours. This frustrates not only those waiting behind you in line, but extra-busy cashiers and baggers, as well. You are less likely to inconvenience other shoppers or the store staff during slower times, like weekday mornings.

Scan magazines at the doctor's offices if they are new for coupons. Most places will not mind if you tear out a coupon if there is not any publications on the other side. Most of the time a magazine is good about only printing coupons on the other side of ads or using tear outs.

Find a store that offers the value of doubling your coupons, to save some serious cash. Even if you need to drive a little further, the money you spend for gas will be well worth the savings you experience at the register when those coupons give you twice the discount.

Signing up for a couponing website is a good idea

so that you can trade with people from other areas. Many companies will print coupons in one area of the country that they do not in others. They are still good nationally, but they may just not be available to you.

A lot of the times you can check one of the bigger named stores you are going to visit online for coupons. You can print out a lot of coupons by doing this and save a lot of money in the process. Just make sure you read the details of the coupons before you use them.

Don't buy an item just because you have a coupon for it. The purpose of using coupons is to save you money. You don't save any money if you ate buying items you don't normally buy. If you do use a coupon for a new item, only buy one to make sure you like it.

A great tip for people who love to use coupons is to print your coupons online. These days, online coupons can result in really amazing savings. Sites like Coupons.com or Coupon Cabin are great sources to find truly great values. You may find savings online that you can't find anywhere else.

When using coupons, it is important to recognize

that small amounts of money add up over time into large amounts. Coupon savings of only 10 or 25 cents may not seem like very much, but you would be surprised at just how much money these small value coupons will end up saving you over your life time. Save little to save big.

Make sure that you pay close attention the expiration date on coupons you are interested in using. If you save them for too long, you may miss the opportunity to use them. It is a good idea to set a reminder in your calendar about a week or two before it expires.

Some of the best coupons that you will find are going to be in your local newspapers. These coupons will be for the stores that are local in your area and very easy to get to, which will improve the level of convenience you have and reduce your stress level.

Trade coupons with your friends or family members. Sometimes it can be worth your time to clip good coupons that you will not be using so that you can trade them with others for coupons that you can use. This helps everyone to save more, and the coupon swaps can offer a fun reason to get together.

If you could, shop at places who offer doubling of coupons. Many stores let you do this and it can save you lots of money. You can get double coupons and get a item for nothing. Getting items free is always more fun! As well, you may be able to test some products you'd never try otherwise.

A good tip you can try out if you're into using coupons is to subscribe to the newsletter of all your favorite stores. This is a win-win scenario because the store is holding onto you as a consumer, and they in turn will provide you with special coupons that you can use.

If you get heavily involved in using coupons, but don't like to spend money printing or buying newspapers, talk to your friends. Many people throw out the coupons from their Sunday papers, and will hold on to them for you to come and collect. Do not try to collect them out of the trash, as this can be illegal.

Ask your friends and family if they know of any cool sites where you can find some discounts. It is always a good thing to share information with other people about where to get discounts that way you can all figure out where to save together. Just remember to always share your secrets with them and things should work out.

When you are clipping coupons always make sure you look on the front and back of each sheet of paper to make sure you are not going to cut into another coupon on accident. Often times the papers make sure that this will not happen by offsetting the coupons, but you will want to double check.

Organize your coupons in a way that makes sense to you. Maybe you want to keep all the coupons for baby things together, and you want to keep all the food coupons together. You might even decide to sort them by brand. However you organize them, make sure you can remember what you've done.

Go to the manufacturer's site directly. Usually you can save a few bucks on your preferred brands by signing up online at your favorite retailer. All you have to do is supply them with your email address, and they will send you some coupons. Since it is a retailer you shop at, getting email from them is something you want.

Shop at stores that multiply coupons. Some stores

double or triple coupons everyday. Other stores have certain days on which they will multiply manufacturer coupons. Be sure to read the fine print, because some stores just allow a limited number to be multiplied, require a minimum purchase, or only multiply coupons with lower values.

To get the most out of your grocery store coupons, know which stores occasionally run double or triple coupon weeks. Talk to the managers of those stores to find out how often they do them. See if you can get wind of when the next one is and be ready.

If your store has a buy one get one free deal you can look for coupons to use on these and you may end up getting two items for free. It is totally worth it to double check the buy one get one free deals your store has to make sure you aren't missing anything.

If you snag a truly great deal with a coupon for an item that you won't use, donate it. Food banks will accept nearly any packaged food item. Women's shelters can often use diapers, shampoo, and other toiletries and supplies. Research and contact local resources in your community to find out what they need, and use your couponing skills for good.

If you're serious about couponing, get organized! Struggling to find the most recent coupons in a messy pile is problematic. If you don't find them quick enough, they can expire. Try keeping your coupons inside some binder-sized sleeve protectors or baseball card holders. These can keep all of your coupons tidy so that you can easily see them and take them to the store with you.

To make your coupon hobby run more smoothly, try purchasing a three-ring binder, and fill it with baseball card collector sheets. Each sheet contains 9 pockets that you can fill with your coupons. Coupons can then be divided into categories, such as cleaning supplies, beauty products and many other categories.

A good coupon tip you can use is to sort you coupons by their expiration date. Organizing your coupons this way will make it so that you get the most out of your coupons and you won't waste any of them. It will make your shopping get done much smoother.

Sign up for the mailing lists of your favorite stores and brands. Many companies send out coupons to people subscribed to their list that aren't available otherwise. Stores also send valuable store-specific coupons like a percentage of your purchase or a dollar amount off a purchase of a certain amount.

Stay away from coupon clipping services. These people claim to charge you only for the time it took to clip coupons, but some manufacturers do not see it that way. It is illegal to buy or sell coupons, and if you are caught, you can be charged with coupon fraud.

Organize your coupons according to the setup of the store. This is a great strategy if you aren't sure which items are on sale. You can easily check the price of the item as you pass by it in the store. If it isn't on sale, move on to the next coupon.

Clipping coupons can save your family a lot of money. All it takes is a little research and dedication, and you will be getting deep discounts at regular national retailers on name brands. You will be shocked at how much you will be able to save on your grocery and toiletry bill.

Get the Sunday newspaper every week. This is by far the easiest way to get access to the most coupons. Check with your local paper, they may have a subscription option that will allow you to get only the Sunday edition. This is often cheaper and more convenient than buying a copy every Sunday.

Using coupons to save money on your grocery bills is a great idea and every Sunday in the newspaper there are lots of them. Sometimes if there are a lot of coupons for items you use frequently, you may want to purchase an additional Sunday paper for the extra coupons.

Before deciding to use a coupon, be sure that you're getting a great deal. It is not uncommon for the generic offerings in the store to hold a better value for your shopping dollar than the coupon can afford you. Coupons do not always garner the best price for what you want.

To make the most out of coupons, combine them with sales. There may be times you need to save a coupon a couple weeks rather than using it when you go shopping next. You might also need to stop at additional stores, but the payoff makes it worthwhile.

Educate yourself before you get started couponing. Know what various terms mean. Become familiar with the policies of your local store. For example, can you use both a store coupon and a manufacturer's coupon on the same item? Does your store double coupons? Understanding the process will save you time and frustration.

Go to the manufacturer's site directly. Usually you can save a few bucks on your preferred brands by signing up online at your favorite retailer. All you have to do is supply them with your email address, and they will send you some coupons. Since it is a retailer you shop at, getting email from them is something you want.

Sign up for a coupon trading circle with other women. You can do this online or in your local area. You will find coupons from places you do not know about and maybe trade away once for items that you are already stocked up on, or that you know you will never use.

Never buy an item simply because you have a great coupon for it. Only buy items you need. If a coupon offers great savings, you may feel tempted to go ahead and use it. Resist that temptation. You're using coupons to save money. Don't waste your income on things you don't even need.

Try to find unused newspapers to avoid spending

extra money that you do not need to. Some retailers are throwing these away every week. The effort it takes to get these extra papers is worth it because you can use the coupons.

If you find a good coupon in your Sunday paper, check local stores and gas stations on Monday morning. They are likely going to still have some extra copies of that paper laying around. Buy them, and you are going to have extra copies of that coupon to use yourself.

A great place to look for coupons are in magazines and newspapers. Sure people may not turn to newspapers and magazines as much as they used to, but they are still a great source for coupons so make sure that you go through them to find the best deals possible.

Use your time efficiently. Coupon clipping takes some time and a little effort but pays off in the end. For best results, be consistent and set up a routine for locating and clipping your coupons. Cut coupons for half a year prior to going to bed every night. You could also reserve some time during your lunch break in order to clip some coupons. Work with the schedule that you have.

Only use coupons on items that are on sale. You can get the most out of your money this way. If an item is not on sale and you buy it just because you have a coupon, you could be wasting money. Hold on to your coupons until the next week when sales change and the item you want is on sale.

A good tip if you're someone that uses coupons is to use a coupon on an item that you'd like to try out. Sometimes we'd like to try out new products but don't want to pay full price for them. Using a coupon will sweeten the deal, and you'll get a chance to try out the product for yourself.

You can use more than one coupon when you are making a purchase, it just has to be of a different item most of the time. Read the fine print to be sure of this, but in theory, you should be able to use a coupon for almost everything that you buy if there's a coupon for it.

Follow the blogs. There is a huge community of couponers online. Many bloggers do the dirty deal-finding work for you and make it super simple to score the deals. They tell you exactly which items are on sale, what corresponding coupons are available, and exactly where to find those coupons.

It is a great way to find the best couponing deals without all the work.

Keep your eye out for coupons in unexpected places. The phone book, the backs of receipts, and newspapers are great places to find these tickets to savings. The coupons in these locations are often for restaurants, mechanics, salons and other experiences or services. There's no reason to limit your coupon usage to grocery shopping!

Find coupons in your magazines. Magazines have always been full of advertisements, but recently advertisers have been adding coupons to many of their magazine ads. Look for tear-out cards with coupons or even coupons printed directly on the page. Even if you aren't planning on reading the magazine right away, when it arrives in the mail, do a quick flip-through to find coupons before their expiration dates pass.

Using coupons to save money on your grocery bills is a great idea and every Sunday in the newspaper there are lots of them. Sometimes if there are a lot of coupons for items you use frequently, you may want to purchase an additional Sunday paper for the extra coupons.

There are many places in which you can look to find coupons. The Sunday paper is often full of coupon flyers. You can also locate the coupons in mailings, grocery store advertisements and in magazines. In addition, certain websites exist that give you the ability to choose your desired coupons and print them.

A great tip when using coupons is to keep track of the expiration date. You don't want to walk into a store, pick up an item and then present the cashier with a coupon that's expired. Some stores might still honor the deal but most won't, and you'll be embarrassed.

Get stacking! Look into your favorite stores' coupon policies. Many stores, like Target, allow you to combine manufacturer and store coupons on one item. So, basically, you can use two coupons on one item. To figure out which type of coupons you have, look in the box located at the top of the coupon near the expiration date.

Many people turn to dumpster diving when they are hungry for more coupons, and this may be a practice you will want to consider if you become desperate. Don't assume that you have to dive headfirst into the dumpster. Just don some gloves and rummage through the papers until you locate some good coupons. You might just be shocked at how many coupons wind up in the trash.

Purchase a good-quality binder for all of your coupons. You will need to purchase several sheet protectors to hold your coupons. In addition to sheet protectors, you will also need dividers to organize your binder. Use these dividers for each type of coupon or each aisle in your grocery store.

Target the smaller sizes on the grocery shelf to maximize your coupon. The reduction in size also carries a reduction in initial price. When you reduce your unit cost, you save more in the long run. This will let you control your usage of products better overall as well.

There is no shame in utilizing coupons. In our tough economy, everyone wants to save money. People are trying many different ways to stretch those paycheck dollars. It is not shameful to want to keep more of your hard-earned money.

Keep your eyes peeled for peelies! When wandering through your local store, be on the lookout for coupons stuck to the outside of products or hanging around the necks of bottles. These are called peelies and hangtags in coupon lingo, and can save you big bucks! Also look for coupon dispensers in aisles to save even more.

Always have your coupons available. The truth is, you never know when you might need to stop and pick something up while you are out. By keeping your coupons either in your vehicle or in your bag, you will always have them readily available should the need to shop arise.

If a product has a mail-in rebate offer, make sure that it is worth the postage and your time. If it is, make certain that you mail it in quickly. Some stores will offer you a special receipt, specifically for rebates. If your store doesn't, pay for the item separately so that you have your receipt for other items.

The first thing you're going to need when approaching using coupons for shopping is to build yourself a coupon binder. This binder will help you stay organized and have an ongoing supply of coupons for each visit. You can stock up on coupons that don't expire for awhile, and you can also stock up on coupons that you use consistently.

If you are couponing to save on groceries, remember that you can't favor brands. You have to be willing to purchase items that are both on sale and that you have coupons for. While it may be okay to keep one or two favorites, in general, you have to be flexible.

Create your shopping list before you go to the store based on the coupons you want to use. You can also use the coupons you have to get ideas on what meals to cook that week. This will help you save time while shopping and make sure you use the coupons you have instead of letting them expire.

Join clubs. Many grocery or department stores offer club savings discounts only for their members. You can get special deals emailed to you or delivered straight to your mailbox simply for signing up. These exclusive coupons can sometimes be combined with other special offers, making it a deal you do not want to pass up.

Organize your coupons. You can purchase coupon organizers and binders at many mass retail chains as well as online stores. You can organize your coupons by subject, or by the expiration date. Each compartment or sleeve can be labeled with the information you need. Another inexpensive option is to place coupons in separate envelopes.

Develop a schedule for your couponing efforts. This can turn into a daily activity, which is fun because you are saving a lot of money. Look through your daily activities and identify times that you can devote to coupons. If you find yourself without any coupons to clip during this time, use the Internet to research new coupon opportunities. Save these sites so you can check them later.

Using coupons to save money on your grocery bills is a great idea and every Sunday in the newspaper there are lots of them. Sometimes if there are a lot of coupons for items you use frequently, you may want to purchase an additional Sunday paper for the extra coupons.

Before beginning any coupon strategy find and print a copy of the store's coupon policy. Many stores limit the number of coupons that can be used on each transaction, while other stores may not accept internet coupons. It is therefore, important that you print a copy of your store's coupon policy.

Create a detailed list when you shop, leveraging off of your coupons. You also have to be sure you have all your coupons on hand so you're able to check items off when you're putting them in the cart. You should also note the quantity of the items you buy.

Take advantage of any reward's cards programs that your local grocery store provides. Often times the store will allow you to load certain coupons right onto your card. This is so nice because you do not have to clip them out, but you also have to remember to note what you put on the card so that you are sure what you need to buy. Furthermore, you cannot use more than one coupon at a time, and they often limit doubling.

Peruse the store ads before you clip your coupons. You could discover that visiting several different stores can result in big savings rather than visiting a single place.

Request all the free sample offers you can find. Not only will you get the free sample in the mail, but often times you'll receive a coupon for the item as well. Coupons that come with free samples tend to be higher value than others, so you'll get a great sample and a great deal!

A great tip you can try if you like to use coupons is to do some comparing from coupons of different stores. This is a good way to find the very best deal. Some stores will even match a competitor's price, which means you won't have to travel all over to different stores.

If you are clipping coupons, add a binder to your list of supplies. A binder is a great way to store and organize your coupons, and you can carry it with you every time you shop. Having it on hand will help to ensure that you use the coupons you clip and save money.

Don't use up all your time collecting coupons. It can take up a whole lot of time clipping and organizing all those coupons. Dedicate no more than an hour or two a week to cut out coupons.

Go ahead and get the Sunday paper so that you can find all of the coupons and discounts that are in them. You can save a lot of money buy paying a few dollars to purchase the Sunday paper for all of the coupons that are inside of it that offer you good deals.

Join like-minded people on forums and social networks to really empower your couponing. Few things are loved by more people and with such passion as saving money, so find a site where people share their tips, codes and strategies to saving more money with the use of money saving coupons.

Compare prices between the warehouse and the grocer. There can often be a better deal waiting for you at the your local 'warehouse' store. Check online or check the prices between the two, in person, and evaluate the best use of your coupons. You may buy a little more, yet save a little more as well.

One key tip for anyone who collects coupons is to never throw away those coupons you get in the mail. You can actually get some great value in these coupons, particularly with fast-food restaurants. Make sure that you at least glance over them before throwing anything away in the garbage.

Try to cut out coupons that you are going to use more often than not. If you use coupons regularly, this will give you a better mindset for cutting them out, which will give you an incentive in the first place. Furthermore, using coupons on items that you need will reduce wasteful spending.

Never buy an item simply because you have a great coupon for it. Only buy items you need. If a coupon offers great savings, you may feel tempted to go ahead and use it. Resist that temptation. You're using coupons to save money. Don't waste your income on things you don't even need.

When you are trying to acquire the best coupons, one of the things that you will need to do is make sure that they are not expired. The worst thing that you can do is spend unnecessary time cutting out coupons that are no longer valid to use on your purchase.

Look for coupons on your favorite items early every month. Most of the time, manufacturers put a cap on the number of coupons available to consumers, and different sites and stores will be allotted different amounts but all around the first week of each month. Make sure you get your savings by checking in early!

* * *